THE WIND THAT SHAKES THE BARLEY

AND OTHER IRISH SONGS OF WAR & REBELLION

Illustrated Edition

JOSHUA HAMPTON

SEVEN CROWNS
PUBLISHING

The Wind That Shakes the Barley
and Other Irish Songs of War & Rebellion

First Edition: November 1, 2019

For more information about this book,
visit **www.JoshuaHampton.com.**

For Mom & Dad

My deepest love and thanks for filling our home with the
sounds of protest music—and unknowingly fostering
my own rebellious nature.

TABLE OF CONTENTS

THE KANDYAN WARS

THE NAPOLEONIC WARS

THE YOUNG IRELANDER REBELLION

THE CRIMEAN WAR

THE AMERICAN CIVIL WAR ERA

THE FENIAN UPRISING

Preface

"Ireland does not rank low in songs. She is far above England, or Italy, or Spain. [...] If men able to write will fling themselves gallantly and faithfully on the work we have here plotted for them, we shall soon have fair and theater, concert hall and drawing-room, road and shop, echoing with songs bringing [...] courage and patriotism to every heart."

Excerpted from The Songs of Ireland, *Edited by Michael Joseph Barry, 1845*

A Note from the Author

Ireland's history of rebellion dates back a millennium. Beginning with the Norman Invasion of 1169, outsiders have done what they might to claim dominion over the wee island and its inhabitants. But no matter the invader, motive, or means, one thing has always proven true—Ireland and its people are not so easily conquered. And from such hardy resilience inevitably is born a most wonderful music to celebrate it.

It would take a voluminous tome to cover even a fraction of the ballads that have originated from Ireland's centuries-long struggle for independence. For this modest volume, I have focused on those songs most widely known, written before the 20th century (to avoid any possible copyright entanglements). And so, sadly, such famous ballads as *The Foggy Dew, Kevin Barry,* and *The Patriot Game* must wait for a possible Volume II.

However, that is not to slight those songs included here. The works within these pages are so much more than the lays of proud poets and balladeers. They are lessons in history, calls to arms, and laments for loved ones lost. But most of all, they are testimonies to the fact that a people's spirit is not so easily broken, no matter the adversity or foe. And to that may many an Irish soul agree.

— Joshua Hampton, July 2019

About the Text

The text of the ballads, but for a very few exceptions, is as it was originally published, including spelling errors and variances in the names of people and places.

Listen as You Read

Visit Spotify for the audio companion to this book, a playlist with recordings of Irish ballads by Bob Dylan, Bruce Springsteen, Sam Lee, the Pogues, Joe Strummer and many more.

Search for The Wind That Shakes the Barley.

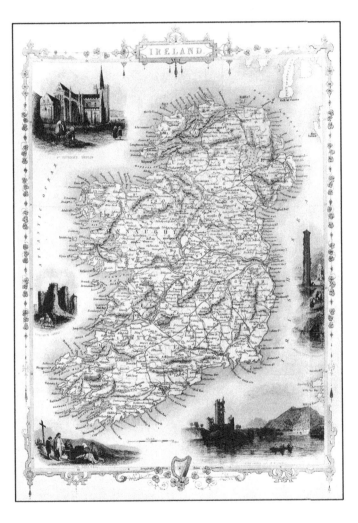

Map of Old Ireland Ireland, 1851

THE DESMOND REBELLIONS

1569-1573 and 1579-1583

Led by the Irish Earldom of Desmond, the Desmond Rebellions were in response to the Elizabethan English state's growing authority over the Irish province of Munster, as well as other factors. The rebellions began after the Earl Gerald of Desmond was jailed, and the Captain General of the Desmond army, James Fitzmaurice, and his allies attacked several English settlements. The English responded by laying waste to towns and castles while indiscriminately killing all civilians they came by. After years of bloodshed, the Earl was released and Fitzmaurice negotiated a pardon, ending the first rebellion.

The second rebellion saw Fitzmaurice again lead insurrections throughout the south until his death in battle, when Gerald the Earl of Desmond assumed leadership. The rebels sacked English-controlled towns, which in return led to the Crown's destruction of Desmond lands. In 1580, clan leader Fiach MacHugh O'Byrne brought the uprising to Leinster in the east. The rebellions at last ended with the Earl of Desmond's death and subsequent surrender of the rebel leaders. When all was done, tens of thousands had died by violence or the resulting famine and bubonic plague.

Carlow Castle, County Carlow, Ireland

Follow Me Up to Carlow

THE STORY: The brother-in-law of famed clan leader Fiach MacHugh O'Byrne is urged to stop lamenting the loss of his land to the Lord Deputy of Ireland, for O'Byrne is on the march to overthrow the British rule. And with so many of the Crown's military commanders sick, wounded or otherwise indisposed, there is no better time to join O'Byrne on the journey to Carlow to fight.

Lift, MacCahir Óg, your face,
Brooding over the old disgrace,
That Black Fitzwilliam stormed your place,
Drove you to the Fern.
Grey said victory was sure,
Soon the firebrand he'd secure;
Until he met at Glenmalure
With Fiach MacHugh O'Byrne.

Curse and swear Lord Kildare,
Fiach will do what Fiach will dare,
Now Fitzwilliam, have a care,
Fallen is your star, low!
Up with halbert out with sword,
On we'll go for by the Lord,

3

THE WIND THAT SHAKES THE BARLEY

Fiach MacHugh has given the word,
Follow me up to Carlow!

See the swords of Glen Imaal,
They're flashing over the English Pale,
See all the children of the Gael,
Beneath O'Byrne's banners.
Rooster of a fighting stock,
Would you let a Saxon cock
Crow out upon an Irish rock?
Fly up and teach him manners!

Curse and swear Lord Kildare,
Fiach will do what Fiach will dare,
Now Fitzwilliam, have a care,
Fallen is your star, low!
Up with halbert out with sword,
On we'll go for by the Lord,
Fiach MacHugh has given the word,
Follow me up to Carlow!

From Tassagart to Clonmore,
There flows a stream of Saxon gore,
O, great is Rory Óg O'More,
At sending the loons to Hades.

White is sick, Lane is fled,
Now for Black Fitzwilliam's head,
We'll send it over dripping red
To Queen Liza and her ladies.

Curse and swear Lord Kildare,
Fiach will do what Fiach will dare,
Now Fitzwilliam, have a care,
Fallen is your star, low!
Up with halbert out with sword,
On we'll go for by the Lord,
Fiach MacHugh has given the word,
Follow me up to Carlow!

SONG NOTES & HISTORY

Follow Me Up to Carlow details the decades of turmoil in Ireland near the end of the 1500's, especially during the second Desmond Rebellion at the Battle of Glenmalure, when clan leader Fiach MacHugh O'Byrne and his men helped to defeat 3,000 English soldiers. The lyric was written by Patrick Joseph McCall and was first published in his collection *Songs of Erinn* in 1899, under the alternate title *Marching Song of Feagh MacHugh*. The tune itself is thought to be a bagpipers' air that O'Byrne and his forces marched to. The song's many obscure references to real people, places and events make it as much a history lesson as a rallying call.

WORDS TO KNOW

MacCahir Óg—Brian MacCahir Óg, O'Byrne's brother-in-law and friend.

Black Fitzwilliam—William Fitzwilliam, Lord Deputy of Ireland.

Grey—Arthur Grey, 14th Baron Grey de Wilton, whose forces were defeated by O'Byrne at the Battle of Glenmalure.

Lord Kildare—Pierce Fitzgerald, the Sheriff of Kildare.

Halbert—A two-handed pole weapon, similar to the pike.

Carlow—The county town of County Carlow.

Glen Imaal, Tassagart and Clonmore—Prominent areas around County Wicklow, where O'Byrne was clan leader.

English Pale—A part of eastern Ireland where the English held dominion as early as 1172.

Gael—A person who speaks Gaelic.

White—Sir Nicholas White, the British military governor of Wexford.

Lane—Sir Ralph Lane, Muster Master General of Ireland.

Rory Óg O'More—A famous Irish rebel and son to another of O'Byrne's brothers-in-law.

Queen Liza—Queen Elizabeth of England.

SELECTED RECORDINGS

The Wolfe Tones, *Follow Me Up to Carlow* (1965)

Planxty, *Follow Me Up to Carlow* (1973)

The Young Dubliners, *Follow Me Up to Carlow* (2007)

The High Kings, *Follow Me Up to Carlow* (2016)

The Kilkennys, *Follow Me Up to Carlow* (2018)

TYRONE'S REBELLION

1593-1603

Tyrone's Rebellion, also called the Nine Years' War, was fought between Irish rebels and British forces in response to the Tudor conquest of Ireland. The Irish Alliance, bolstered by Spanish troops, was largely led by Red Hugh O'Donnell of the Gaelic kingdom of Tyrconnell, along with Hugh O'Neill, the Earl of Tyrone. With more than 18,000 British troops involved, it was the largest English conflict during Queen Elizabeth's reign.

After nearly a decade of bitter fighting all over the country, O'Donnell and O'Neill were at last forced into exile after the decisive British victory at the Battle of Kinsale. The war concluded with the Treaty of Mellifont, which officially ended the centuries-old empire of Gaelic Ireland.

The Battle of Yellow Ford, 1598

O'Donnell Abú

THE STORY: The Clan O'Donnell, led by the renowned warrior chief Red Hugh, is called to assemble its forces to fight the tyrannical English.

Proudly the note of the trumpet is sounding;
Loudly the war cries arise on the gale;
Fleetly the steed by Lough Swilly is bounding,
To join the thick squadrons on Saimear's green vale.
On, ev'ry mountaineer,
Strangers to flight or fear,
Rush to the standard of dauntless Red Hugh.
Bonnaught and Gallowglass,
Throng from each mountain pass.
On for old Erin, "O'Donnell Abú!"

Princely O'Neill to our aid is advancing,
With many a chieftain and warrior clan.
A thousand proud steeds in his vanguard are prancing,
'Neath the borderers brave from the banks of the Bann:
Many a heart shall quail
Under its coat of mail.
Deeply the merciless foeman shall rue
When on his ears shall ring,

Borne on the breeze's wing,
Tír Chonaill's dread war-cry, "O'Donnell Abú!"

Wildly o'er Desmond the war-wolf is howling;
Fearless the eagle sweeps over the plain;
The fox in the streets of the city is prowling—
All who would scare them are banished or slain!
Grasp ev'ry stalwart hand,
Hackbut and battle brand—
Pay them all back the debt so long due;
Norris and Clifford well
Can of Tirconnell tell;
Onward to glory—"O'Donnell Abú!"

Sacred the cause that Clan Connell's defending—
The altars we kneel at and homes of our sires;
Ruthless the ruin the foe is extending—
Midnight is red with the plunderers' fires.
On with O'Donnell then,
Fight the old fight again,
Sons of Tirconnell,
All valiant and true:
Make the proud Saxon feel
Erin's avenging steel!
Strike for your country! "O'Donnell Abú!"

THE WIND THAT SHAKES THE BARLEY

SONG NOTES & HISTORY

Originally called *The Clan Connell War Song*, this triumphant call to arms was written by Michael Joseph McCann and first printed in *The Nation* in 1843. The lyric refers to Red Hugh O'Donnell, a clan chief who ruled the Irish kingdom Tyrconnell in the late sixteenth century and rebelled against the Crown during Tyrone's Rebellion. In Gaelic, Abú means "onward", a rallying cry which followed a commander's name. The song appears in the 1966 Walt Disney live-action film *The Fighting Prince of Donegal*.

WORDS TO KNOW

Lough Swilly—A sea inlet in County Donegal.

Saimear—An old name for the town of Ballyshannon, the site of a famous victory by Red Hugh O'Donnell.

Bonnaught and Gallowglass—Irish and Scottish mercenaries who guarded the mountain passes for O'Donnell.

Erin—The Irish word for Ireland.

Princely O'Neill—Refers to Hugh O'Neill, the Earl of Tyrone, who allied his family and forces with O'Donnell during the Nine Year's War.

The Bann—The longest river in Northern Ireland.

Tír Chonaill—The Gaelic spelling of the kingdom covering much of what is now County Donegal.

Desmond—A historic kingdom in southwestern Ireland.

Hackbut and Battle Brand—A muzzle-loaded long gun and fighting sword.

Norris—Sir John Norris, the most acclaimed English soldier of his day.

Clifford—Sir Conyers Clifford, an English political and military commander.

SELECTED RECORDINGS

The Clancy Brothers & Tommy Makem,
O'Donnell Abú (1956)

Wylde Nept, *O'Donnell Abú* (2006)

THE WILLIAMITE WAR IN IRELAND

1689-1691

The Williamite War in Ireland, also known as the Jacobite War in Ireland or The War of the Two Kings, was fought between the supporters of the Catholic King James II (who were known as the Jacobites) and the supporters of the Dutch Protestant Prince William of Orange (known as the Williamites) over who would become monarch of the kingdoms of England, Scotland and Ireland.

The Irish Catholics, with military assistance from the French, largely supported King James, while the Irish Protestants, English, Scottish, Danish and Dutch mostly fought for Prince William. As the majority in Ireland, the Jacobites secured most of the country's towns and cities in the name of King James. However, they suffered successive, decisive defeats at the Battles of Boyne and Aughrim in 1690 and 1691, which led to the war's end, though the Jacobites would continue their rebellious efforts in a series of sporadic uprisings until 1746.

The Battle of Boyne in the Williamite War, 1690

Jackets Green

THE STORY: A young Irish woman falls for a Jacobite soldier in his handsome green uniform. When the soldier is killed in battle, the woman laments the loss of her beloved and urges other maidens to love Irish soldiers above all.

When I was a maiden fair and young,
On the pleasant banks of Lee,
No bird that in the greenwood sung,
Was half so light and free.
My heart ne'er beat with flying feet,
No love sang me his queen,
Till down the glen rode Sarsfield's men,
And they wore the jackets green.

Young Dhonal sat on his gallant grey
Like a king on a royal seat,
And my heart leaped out on his regal way
To worship at his feet.
O Love, had you come in those colours dressed,
And wooed with a soldier's mien
I'd have laid my head on your throbbing breast
For the sake of your jacket green.

No hoarded wealth did my love own,
Save the good sword that he bore;
But I loved him for himself alone
And the colour bright he wore.
For had he come in England's red
To make me England's queen,
I'd rove the high green hills instead
For the sake of the Irish green.

When William stormed with shot and shell
At the walls of Garryowen,
In the breach of death my Dhonal fell,
And he sleeps near the Treaty Stone.
That breach the foeman never crossed
While he swung his broadsword keen;
But I do not weep my darling lost,
For he fell in his jacket green.

When Sarsfield sailed away I wept
As I heard the wild ocean.
I felt then dead as the men who slept
'Neath the fields of Garryowen.
While Ireland held my Dhonal blessed,
No wild sea rolled between,
I still could fold him to my breast
All robed in his Irish green.

THE WIND THAT SHAKES THE BARLEY

My soul has sobbed like waves of woe,
That sad o'er tombstones break,
For I buried my heart in his grave below,
For his and for Ireland's sake.
And I cry, "Make way for the soldier's bride
In your halls of death, sad queen,
For I long to rest by my true love's side
And wrapped in the folds of green."

I saw the Shannon's purple tide
Roll by the Irish town,
As I stood in the breach by Dhonal's side
When England's flag went down.
And now it lowers when I seek the skies,
Like a blood red curse between.
I weep, but 'tis not women's sighs
Will raise our Irish green.

Oh, Ireland, sad is thy lonely soul,
And loud beats the winter sea,
But sadder and higher the wild waves roll
O'er the hearts that break for thee.
Yet grief shall come to our heartless foes,
And their thrones in the dust be seen,

So, Irish maids, love none but those
Who wear the jackets green.

SONG NOTES & HISTORY

This broadside ballad was written by Michael Scanlan around 1867. The soldier in the song fights with the Jacobite Army of Irish Commander Patrick Sarsfield in the Williamite War. The song is no. 9520 in the Roud Folk Song Index.

WORDS TO KNOW

Lee—A river that runs through County Cork and empties into the Celtic Sea.

Garryowen—A town outside the city of Limerick and scene of a heroic Jacobite victory during the Williamite War.

Treaty Stone—A block of limestone in Limerick upon which the Treaty of Limerick was signed, ending the Williamite War.

Shannon—The longest river in Ireland.

SELECTED RECORDINGS

Mary O'Hara, *Jackets Green* (1958)

Eileen Donaghy, *Jackets Green* (1960)

The Wolfe Tones, *Jackets Green* (1976)

Liam Donnelly, *Jackets Green* (2008)

Sarah Makem, *Jackets Green* (2012)

THE BATTLE
OF RAMILLIES

May 23, 1706

Fought in Belgium as part of the War of the Spanish Succession, the Battle of Ramillies saw the Grand Alliance forces of Austria, England and the Dutch Republic take on the army of King Louis XIV of France, which was supported by the Irish regiment known as Clare's Dragoons. The Allied forces led by renowned British military commander John Churchill, 1st Duke of Marlborough, defeated the French, leading to the eventual Allied capture of much of the Spanish Netherlands.

The Battle of Ramillies, 1706

Clare's Dragoons

THE STORY: Before the French army's imminent defeat at the Battle of Ramillies, a unit of exiled Irish soldiers known as Clare's Dragoons joins the fray and successfully repels the onslaught of English, Dutch and Danish forces. To spur the dragoons' greatest triumph, their colonel—and son of the unit's first commander—leads the charge before being killed himself, setting a proud example for all brave and determined Irish soldiers to follow.

When on Ramillies' bloody field,
The baffled French were forced to yield,
The victor Saxon backward reeled
Before the charge of Clare's Dragoons.

The flags we conquered in that fray,
Look lone in Ypres' choir, they say,
We'll win them company to-day
Or bravely die like Clare's Dragoons.

Viva la, for Ireland's wrong!
Viva la, for Ireland's right!
Viva la in battle throng,
For a Spanish steed, and sabre bright!

THE WIND THAT SHAKES THE BARLEY

The brave old Lord died near the fight,
But, for each drop he lost that night,
A Saxon cavalier shall bite
The dust before Lord Clare's Dragoons.

For never when our spurs were set
And never, when our sabres met,
Could we the Saxon soldiers get
To stand the shock of Clare's Dragoons.

   Viva la, the New Brigade!
   Viva la, the Old One too!
   Viva la, the rose shall fade,
   And the shamrock shine forever new!

Another Clare is here to lead,
The worthy son of such a breed;
The French expect some famous deed
When Clare leads on his bold Dragoons.

Our Colonel comes from Brian's race,
His wounds are in his breast and face,
The Bearna Baoghail is still his place,
The foremost of his bold Dragoons.

Viva la, the New Brigade!
Viva la, the Old One too!
Viva la, the rose shall fade,
And the shamrock shine forever new!

There's not a man in squadron here
Was ever known to flinch or fear;
Though first in charge and last in rear
Have ever been Lord Clare's Dragoons.

But, see! We'll soon have work to do,
To shame our boasts, or prove them true,
For hither comes the English crew
To sweep away Lord Clare's Dragoons.

Viva la, for Ireland's wrong!
Viva la, for Ireland's right!
Viva la in battle throng,
For a Spanish steed, and sabre bright!

Oh! Comrades! Think how Ireland pines,
Her exiled Lords, her rifled shrines,
Her dearest hope, the ordered lines
And bursting charge of Clare's Dragoons!

THE WIND THAT SHAKES THE BARLEY

The fling your Green Flag to the sky,
Be "Limerick!" your battle cry,
And charge, till blood floats fetlock-high
Around the track of Clare's Dragoons!

Viva la, the New Brigade!
Viva la, the Old One too!
Viva la, the rose shall fade,
And the shamrock shine forever new!

SONG NOTES & HISTORY

Written by Thomas Osborne Davis, *Clare's Dragoons* was
first published in *The Nation* around 1840. The song is a
tribute to the units of exiled Irish fighters who served under
Daniel O'Brien, 3rd Viscount Clare, in the Jacobite War, as
well as his son, Charles, in the War of the Spanish Succession.
During the U.S. Civil War, the ballad's lyric was changed to
celebrate the 12th Regiment of the New York State Militia.

WORDS TO KNOW

Ramillies—A town in Belgium, the site of the famous Battle of Ramillies during the War of the Spanish Succession.

Ypres' Choir—The section of a church between the nave and the altar where military or historical flags are sometimes displayed.

Bearna Baoghail—Loosely translates to "the Gap of Danger", a term to describe the Three Bullet Gate in Wexford, a key site in the Battle of New Ross.

Fetlock—The joints of a horse's leg above the hoof.

SELECTED RECORDINGS

Na Casaidigh, *Clare's Dragoons* (1992)

Dick Hogan, *Clare's Dragoons* (2013)

THE IRISH REBELLION OF 1798

May 24, 1798 - October 12, 1798

In May of 1798, The United Irishmen, a Republican group heavily influenced by French and American revolutionaries, led an insurrection aimed at overthrowing British rule of Ireland and establishing a new republic. Over the next three months, the Irish rebels—assisted on occasion by the French army— engaged British, militia and yeomanry troops in the counties of Carlow, Meath, Kildare, Wexford and Wicklow.

Though there were notable rebel victories, mostly in County Wexford, the rebels were overmatched and underprepared. Due to the loss of leadership and the overwhelming number of British Crown forces, the rebellion was ended by Autumn though guerrilla campaigns persisted until the early 1800s. It is estimated between 15,000-30,000 combatants and civilians lost their lives during the conflict. Thousands more rebels were jailed, exiled or executed.

The Last Journey of Father Murphy

Boolavogue

THE STORY: A parish priest leads a band of Wexford rebels to battle the British army. The rebels successfully beat back the British in several skirmishes before ultimately being defeated at Vinegar Hill, after which the priest is captured and executed.

At Boolavogue as the sun was setting
O'er the bright May meadows of Shelmalier,
A rebel hand set the heather blazing
And brought the neighbours from far and near.

Then Father Murphy from old Kilcormack
Spurred up the rocks with a warning cry:
'Arm! Arm!' he cried, 'For I've come to lead you;
For Ireland's freedom we'll fight or die!'

He led us on against the coming soldiers,
And the cowardly yeomen we put to flight:
'Twas at the Harrow the boys of Wexford
Showed Bookey's regiment how men could fight.

Look out for hirelings, King George of England;
Search every kingdom where breathes a slave,

For Father Murphy of County Wexford
Sweeps o'er the land like a mighty wave.

We took Camolin and Enniscorthy
And Wexford storming drove out our foes,
'Twas at Slieve Coilte our pikes were reeking
With the crimson blood of the beaten Yeos.

At Tubberneering and Ballyellis
Full many a Hessian lay in his gore,
Ah! Father Murphy had aid come over
The green flag floated from shore to shore!

At Vinegar Hill, o'er the pleasant Slaney,
Our heroes vainly stood back to back,
and the Yeos at Tullow took Father Murphy
and burned his body upon a rack.

God grant you glory, brave Father Murphy,
And open Heaven to all your men,
The cause that called you may call tomorrow
In another fight for the Green again.

SONG NOTES & HISTORY

Boolavogue, which takes its name from a village near Enniscorthy in County Wexford, tells the true story of Father John Murphy and his army of Wexford rebels during the Irish Rebellion of 1798. Written by Patrick Joseph McCall, it was first published in *The Irish Independent* in 1898 to celebrate the Rebellion's 100th anniversary. It was originally titled *Fr. Murphy of the County Wexford*.

WORDS TO KNOW

Boolavogue—A village northeast of Enniscorthy in County Wexford.

Shelmalier—A barony of County Wexford.

Father Murphy—Father John Murphy, an Irish Catholic priest and leader of the Wexford Rebellion during the 1798 uprising.

Kilcormack—A small town in County Offaly.

The Harrow—The Battle of the Harrow, the first clash between rebels and British troops in County Wexford.

Wexford—The county town of County Wexford, and site of many key events during the 1798 Rebellion.

Bookey—Thomas Bookey, a lieutenant of the Camolin cavalry whose death at the Battle of the Harrow was a flashpoint for the Wexford Rebellion.

Camolin—A town in County Wexford, known for the yeomanry cavalry unit drawn from the village.

Enniscorthy—A large town located in County Wexford and the site of many battles during the 1798 Rebellion.

Slieve Coilte—A high hill in County Wexford where the rebels camped.

Tubberneering—A town in County Wexford and site of the famous rebel victory, the Battle of Tubberneering.

Ballyellis—The Battle of Ballyellis, a victory for the rebels near the town of Ballyellis, County Wicklow.

Hessians—German troops hired by the British to fight during the Revolutionary War and Irish Rebellion of 1798.

Vinegar Hill—The headquarters of the rebels who controlled Wexford for thirty days during the rebellion.

Slaney—The River Slaney in southeast Ireland.

Yeos—Volunteer British troops whose ranks were drawn from Irish nobility, landed gentry, and their tenants.

Tullow—A market town in County Carlow, where Father Murphy was betrayed, captured and executed.

SELECTED RECORDINGS

The Clancy Brothers & Tommy Makem,
Boolavogue (1956)

The Dubliners, *Boolavogue* (1976)

The Irish Tenors, *Boolavogue* (2010)

Dermot O'Brien, *Boolavogue* (2008)

Dick Hogan, *Boolavogue* (2013)

Patrick Feeney, *Boolavogue* (2015)

Badge of the Society of United Irishmen

The Boys of Wexford

THE STORY: A captain's daughter offers a rebel from Wexford a thousand pounds to convince him to leave home to fight for Ireland's freedom. She also offers to disguise herself as a man and follow him. The rebel declines her offers yet still pledges himself to both her and the cause. He then recounts various battles of the rebellion, mentioning a few proud victories as well as several unfortunate defeats he blames on the rebels' excessive drinking.

> In comes the captain's daughter,
> the captain of the Yeos,
> Saying, "Brave United man,
> we'll ne'er again be foes.
> A thousand pounds I'll give you,
> and fly from home with thee
> And dress myself in man's attire,
> and fight for liberty!"

> We are the boys of Wexford,
> who fought with heart and hand
> To burst in twain the galling chain,
> and free our native land!

"I want no gold, my maiden fair,
to fly from home with thee;
Your shining eyes will be my prize,
more dear than gold to me.
I want no gold to nerve my arm
to do a true man's part
To free my land I'd gladly give
the red drops from my heart."

We are the boys of Wexford,
who fought with heart and hand
To burst in twain the galling chain,
and free our native land!

And when we left our cabins, boys,
we left with right good will,
To see our friends and neighbours
that were at Vinegar Hill!
A young man from our ranks,
a cannon he let go;
He slapt it into Lord Mountjoy,
a tyrant he laid low!

We are the boys of Wexford,
who fought with heart and hand

THE WIND THAT SHAKES THE BARLEY

> To burst in twain the galling chain,
> and free our native land!

We bravely fought and conquered
at Ross, and Wexford town;
And if we failed to keep them,
'twas drink that brought us down.
We had no drink beside us
on Tubberneering's day,
Depending on the long bright pike,
and well it worked its way!

> We are the boys of Wexford,
> who fought with heart and hand
> To burst in twain the galling chain,
> and free our native land!

They came into the country
our blood to waste and spill;
But let them weep for Wexford,
and think of Oulart Hill!
'Twas drink that still betrayed us,
of them we had no fear;
For every man could do his part
like Forth and Shelmalier!

> We are the boys of Wexford,
> who fought with heart and hand
> To burst in twain the galling chain,
> and free our native land!

My curse upon all drinking!
It made our hearts full sore:
For bravery won each battle,
but drink lost ever more.
And if, for want of leaders,
we lost at Vinegar Hill,
We're ready for another fight,
and love our country still!

> We are the boys of Wexford,
> who fought with heart and hand
> To burst in twain the galling chain,
> and free our native land!

SONG NOTES & HISTORY

The Boys of Wexford documents the Wexford Rebellion, which was part of the larger Irish Rebellion of 1798. It was partially written by Robert Dwyer Joyce with music by Arthur Warren Darley, and by all accounts first published in 1873. Joyce said that he had heard the song as a child, but only incorporated two of the original verses into the version he published. When President Kennedy, whose ancestors were Wexford natives, visited Ireland in 1963 a group of school children performed the ballad for him to his great delight. The song is no. 3015 in the Roud Folk Song Index.

WORDS TO KNOW

United Men—The Society of United Irishmen, a revolutionary Republican organization who began the Irish Rebellion of 1798.

Wexford—The county town of County Wexford, and site of many key events during the 1798 Rebellion.

Vinegar Hill—The headquarters of the rebels who controlled Wexford for thirty days during the rebellion.

Lord Mountjoy—Luke Gardiner, 1st Viscount Mountjoy, commander of the British Crown forces, killed during the rebellion at the battle of New Ross in Wexford.

Ross—The Wexford town of New Ross, where the rebels were gravely defeated, halting the spread of the rebellion into County Kilkenny.

Tubberneering—A town in County Wexford and site of the famous rebel victory, the Battle of Tubberneering.

Oulart Hill—The Battle of Oulart Hill, in which a rebel gathering massacred a detachment of North Cork militia.

Forth and Shelmalier—Baronies of County Wexford, both hotbeds of rebel activity during the 1798 Rebellion.

SELECTED RECORDINGS

The Wolfe Tones, *The Boys of Wexford* (1965)

The Clancy Brothers, *The Boys of Wexford* (1995)

The Dublin Boys, *The Boys from Wexford* (2013)

Defeat of the Rebels at Vinegar Hill

Come All You Warriors

THE STORY: The Wexford rebels, led by parish priest
Father Murphy, beat back a corps of British cavalry and several
detachments of militia. They then take the towns of
Enniscorthy and Tubberneering before seeing defeat due to a
lack of expected reinforcements from the French.

Come all you warriors and renowned nobles,
Give ear unto my warlike theme,
While I relate how brave Father Murphy,
He lately roused from his sleepy dream,
Sure Julius Caesar nor Alexander,
Nor brave King Arthur ever equalled him,
For armies formidable he did conquer,
Though with two pikemen he did begin.

Camolin cavalry he did unhorse them,
Their first lieutenant he cut him down,
With shattered ranks and with broken columns,
They soon returned to Camolin town,
At the hill of Oulart he displayed his valour,
Where a hundred Corkmen lay on the plain,
At Enniscorthy his sword he wielded,
And I hope to see him once more again.

THE WIND THAT SHAKES THE BARLEY

When Enniscorthy became subject unto him,
Twas then to Wexford we marched our men,
And on the Three Rock took up our quarters,
Waiting for daylight the town to win,
The loyal townsmen gave their assistance,
We will die or conquer they all did say,
The yeomen cavalry made no resistance,
For on the pavement their corpses lay.

With drums a-beating the town did echo,
And acclamations came from door to door,
On the Windmill Hill we pitched our tents then,
We drank like heroes but paid no score,
On Carraig Rua for some time we waited,
And next to Gorey we did repair,
At Tubberneering we thought no harm,
The bloody army was waiting there.

The issue of it was a close engagement,
While on the soldiers we played warlike pranks,
Through the sheepwalks, hedgerows and shady thickets,
There were mangled bodies and broken ranks,
The shuddering cavalry, I can't forget them,
We raised the brushes on their helmets straight,
They turned about and made straight for Dublin,
As though they ran for a ten-pound plate.

Some crossed Donnybrook and more through Blackrock,
And some up Shankhill without wound or flaw,
And if Barry Lawless be not a liar,
There was more went groaning up Luggala,
To the Windmill Hill of Enniscorthy,
The British Fencibles they fled like deers,
But our ranks were tattered and sorely scattered,
By the loss o Kyan and his Shelmaliers.

The streets of England were left quite naked,
Of all their army both foot and horse,
The Highlands Scotland were left unguarded,
Likewise the Hessians the seas did cross,
But if the Frenchmen had reinforced us,
And landed transports at Baginbun,
Father John Murphy, he would be their seconder,
And sixteen thousand with him would come.

Success attend you sweet County Wexford,
Threw off the yoke and to battle run,
Let them not think we gave up our arms,
For every man still has a pike and gun.

SONG NOTES & HISTORY

Also known as *Father Murphy*, this ballad details the exploits of Wexford rebel leader Father Murphy in the Irish Rebellion of 1798. While its initial publication date is unknown, it most certainly was written soon after the Rebellion itself. The song served as one of the key inspirations for Patrick Joseph McCall's *Boolavogue* one hundred years later.

WORDS TO KNOW

Camolin Cavalry—A mounted cavalry unit made up of volunteers from around the town of Camolin, County Wexford.

Oulart—A small village in County Wexford and the site of the Battle of Oulart Hill in the 1798 Rebellion.

Corkmen—Men from Cork, Ireland.

Enniscorthy—A large town located in County Wexford and the site of many battles during the 1798 Rebellion.

Three Rock—Three Rocks Mountain, also known as Forth Mountain.

Windmill Hill—Another name for Vinegar Hill, the headquarters of the rebels who controlled Wexford for thirty days during the rebellion.

Carraig Rua—Carrigrew Hill, near the town of Gorey, where rebels gathered before defeating the British forces at Tubberneering.

Gorey—A town in north County Wexford.

Tubberneering—A town in County Wexford and site of the famous rebel victory, the Battle of Tubberneering.

Donnybrook & Blackrock—Districts on the southside of Dublin, Ireland.

Shankhill—An area south of Dublin.

Barry Lawless—Possibly a reference to John Lawless, a leader of the United Irishmen.

Luggala—A mountain in the Wicklow Mountains, also known as Fancy Mountain.

British Fencibles—British regiments often composed of local recruits.

47

Kyan & His Shelmaliers—A reference to Esmonde Kyan, a one-armed rebel commander, and his men from the Shelmalier area of County Wexford.

Hessians—German troops hired by the British to fight during the Revolutionary War and Irish Rebellion of 1798.

Baginbun—A headland in County Wexford where the rebels expected reinforcements from the French, who never arrived.

SELECTED RECORDINGS

Frank Harte and Dónal Lunny, *Father Murphy* (1998)

Jerry O'Reilly, *Father Murphy* (2014)

British Soldiers Half-hanging an Irish Rebel

The Croppy Boy

THE STORY: A young Irish rebel is captured by the British and condemned to hang. On his way to the scaffold, he is renounced by his family, who leave him to die.

It was early, early in the spring,
The birds did whistle and sweetly sing,
Changing their notes from tree to tree,
And the song they sang was old Ireland free.

It was early, early in the night,
The yeoman cavalry gave me a fright,
The yeoman cavalry was my downfall,
And taken was I by Lord Cornwall.

'Twas in the guard-house where I was laid,
And in a parlour where I was tried,
My sentence passed and my courage low,
When to Dungannon I was forced to go.

As I pass'd my father's door,
My brother William stood at the door,
My aged father stood at the door,
And my tender mother her hair she tore.

As I was walking up Wexford Street,
My own first cousin I chanced to meet,
My own first cousin did me betray,
And for one bare guinea swore my life away.

My sister Mary heard the express,
She ran up the stairs in her mourning dress,
Five hundred guineas I will lay down,
To see my brother through Wexford town.

As I was walking up Wexford Hill,
Who could blame me to cry my fill?
I looked behind, and I looked before,
But my aged mother I shall see no more.

And as I mounted the platform high,
My aged father was standing by,
My aged father did me deny,
And the name he gave me was the Croppy Boy.

It was in Dungannon this young man died,
And in Dungannon his body lies,
And you good people that do pass by,
Oh, shed a tear for the Croppy Boy.

SONG NOTES & HISTORY

The Croppy Boy first appeared on broadsides shortly after the Irish Rebellion of 1798. The title references a term derived from the short-cropped haircuts worn by many Irish rebels. The song is close in plot and theme to the popular Child ballad *The Maid Freed from the Gallows*. An alternate, more literary version, in which the Croppy Boy is tricked by a British soldier disguised as a priest, was first published in 1845 by Irish poet William B. McBurney. It is also prominently featured in James Joyce's classic novel *Ulysses*. The song is no. 1030 in the Roud Folk Song Index.

WORDS TO KNOW

Lord Cornwall—British General Charles Cornwallis, the 1st Marquess Cornwallis, who was given specific authority to put down the Irish Rebellion of 1798.

Dungannon—A town in County Tyrone.

SELECTED RECORDINGS

The Clancy Brothers & Tommy Makem,
The Croppy Boy (1956)

Ted & Bet Porter, *The Croppy Boy* (1965)

Nic Jones, *The Croppy Boy* (1967)

The Dubliners, *The Croppy Boy* (1967)

The Wolfe Tones, *Croppy Boy* (1987)

Louis Killen, *The Croppy Boy* (1993)

Frank Harte, *The Croppy Boy* (1998)

Henry Munro, Chief of the Irish Rebels

General Munro

THE STORY: An Irish rebel tells the story of General Munro, who fought bravely at the Battle of Ballynahinch. While recovering from the fight, Munro is betrayed by a woman and captured by the British army, who jail and hang him. His sister then vows to avenge his death.

My name is George Campbell, my age is sixteen,
I joined the United Men to fight for the green,
And many's the battle I did undergo,
When commanded by that hero old General Munro.

Were you at the battle of Ballynahinch,
When the people oppressed, rose up in defence,
And Munro took the mountains, his men took the field,
And they fought for three hours and never did yield?

Munro being weary and in need of some sleep,
Gave a woman ten guineas, his secret to keep,
But she got the money, the divil tempted her so,
And she sent for the army and surrendered Munro.

Well, the army, they came and surrounded them all,
He thought to escape but he could not at all,

THE WIND THAT SHAKES THE BARLEY

And they marched him to Lisburn without more delay,
And they hung our poor hero the very same day.

Were you at the farm when the cavalry came there?
How the horses did caper and prance in the rear,
And the traitor being with them as you may all know,
It was out of a haystack they hauled poor Munro.

In came Munro's sister, she was well dressed in green,
She'd a sword by her side that was long, sharp and keen,
Three cheers she did give and away she did go,
Saying I'll have revenge for my brother Munro.

Munro being taken and led to the tree,
Says farewell to my comrades wheresoever they may be,
There's one thing that grieves me and it's parting them so,
So farewell to that hero old General Munro!

SONG NOTES & HISTORY

Also known as *General Monroe*, *General Monro* and *General Munroe*, this broadside ballad memorializes the exploits of

United Irishman Henry Munro, a shopkeeper who led a band of rebels in the losing battle of Ballynahinch during the Irish Rebellion of 1798. It was first published very near to the date of Munro's hanging. Though the song tells of a woman's treachery leading to Munro's capture, he was actually betrayed by a farmer who was hiding him in a pig house. The song is no. 1166 in the Roud Folk Song Index.

WORDS TO KNOW

Ballynahinch—A town in County Down which was sacked and burned by the victorious British following a two-day battle against the rebels.

Lisburn—Munro's hometown in Northern Ireland.

SELECTED RECORDINGS

The Wolfe Tones, *General Munroe* (1978)

Andy Irvine, *General Munroe* (1980)

The Makem Brothers, *General Monroe* (1997)

Frank Harte and Dónal Lunny, *General Munro* (1998)

Declan Hunt, *General Munro* (2016)

Theobald Wolfe Tone

The Grave of Wolfe Tone

THE STORY: A visitor to an Irish rebel leader's grave mourns the loss of such heroes but is heartened by an old man who says soon the grave will be made a monument once Ireland is free from tyranny.

In Bodenstown Churchyard there lies a green grave,
And wildly along it the winter winds rave;
Small shelter I ween on the ruined walls there,
When the storm sweeps down o'er the plains of Kildare.

Once I lay on that spot that lies over Wolfe Tone,
I thought how he perished in prison alone,
His friends unavenged and his country unfreed;
"Oh, bitter," I said, "is the patriot's meed."

There were students and peasants, the wise and the brave,
And the old man who knew him from cradle to grave,
And the children who thought of me hard-hearted, for they
On that sanctified sod were forbidden to play.

But the old man who saw I was mourning there said:
"We've come, sir, to weep where young Wolfe Tone
    is laid,
We're going to raise him a monument, too,
A plain one, yet fit for the simple and true."

In Bodenstown Churchyard there lies a green grave,
And freely around it the winter winds rave.
Far better they suit him the ruin and the gloom,
Until Ireland, a nation, can build him a tomb.

SONG NOTES & HISTORY

The Grave of Wolfe Tone, also known as *Bodenstown Churchyard* or *Tone's Grave*, was written by Young Irelander Thomas Davis and first published in *The Nation* in 1843. Davis wrote it after visiting the unmarked grave of Wolfe Tone, one of the leaders of the Irish Rebellion of 1798, and finding it fiercely guarded by a local blacksmith. The ballad is no. 9313 in the Roud Folk Song Index.

WORDS TO KNOW

Bodenstown Churchyard—A cemetery in County Kildare known for the medieval castle ruins on its grounds.

Kildare—The town from which County Kildare's name was derived.

SELECTED RECORDINGS

The Makem Brothers, *Bodenstown Churchyard* (1997)

The Wolfe Tones, *Bodenstown Churchyard* (2003)

Declan Hunt, *The Grave of Wolfe Tone* (2008)

Frank Harte and Dónal Lunny,
Bodenstown Churchyard (2009)

Liz Hanley, *Bodenstown Churchyard* (2013)

Tom Donovan, *The Grave of Wolfe Tone* (2014)

Massacre by Irish Rebels of Irish Loyalists
on the Wexford Bridge

Kelly the Boy from Killanne

THE STORY: A rebel from Wexford is asked for news of the fight for freedom. He responds that they are preparing to march north, led by the legendary United Man John Kelly, who's said to be a giant with golden hair. News also tells that the rebels have taken two loyalist towns and have a cannon ready for their attack on another the next morning. However, all does not go as planned when the rebels are betrayed and Kelly is killed.

What's the news, what's the news,
Oh my bold Shelmalier,
With your long barreled guns from the sea?
Say what wind from the south
Brings a messenger here
With the hymn of the dawn for the free?
Goodly news, goodly news
Do I bring youth of Forth,
Goodly news shall you hear, Bargy man,
For the boys march at dawn
From the south to the north,
Led by Kelly the boy from Killanne.

THE WIND THAT SHAKES THE BARLEY

Tell me who is that giant
With the gold curling hair,
He who rides at the head of your band?
Seven feet is his height
With some inches to spare,
And he looks like a king in command.
Ah, my boys, that's the pride
Of the bold Shelmaliers,
'Mongst greatest of heroes a man,
Fling your beavers aloft
And give three ringing cheers
For John Kelly the boy from Killanne.

Enniscorthy's in flames
And old Wexford is won
And tomorrow the Barrow we will cross
On a hill o'er the town
We have planted a gun
That will batter the gateway to Ross,
All the Forth men and Bargy men
Will march o'er the heath
With brave Harvey to lead in the van,
But the foremost of all
In that grim gap of death
Will be Kelly the boy from Killanne.

But the gold sun of freedom
Grew darkened at Ross,
And it set by the Slaney's red waves,
And poor Wexford stripped naked,
Hung high on a cross,
With her heart pierced by traitors and slaves,
Glory-o, glory-o
To her brave sons who died
For the cause of long down trodden man,
Glory-o to Mount Leinster's own darling and pride,
Dauntless Kelly the boy from Killanne.

SONG NOTES & HISTORY

Written by Patrick Joseph McCall and first published in his 1911 collection *Irish Fireside Songs*, this ballad commemorates the exploits of the famous United Irish leader John Kelly who fought in the 1798 Rebellion. While wounded he was captured in the town of Wexford, then tried and hanged by the British. Stories say he was also decapitated and his head kicked about the street before being displayed on a pike.

WORDS TO KNOW

Shelmalier—A rebel from the Shelmalier area of County Wexford.

Forth—A barony of County Wexford.

Bargy Man—A man from the barony of Bargy in County Wexford.

Killane—A town in the parish of Rathnure, County Wexford.

Beavers—Slang for the beaver hats popular in the 18th century.

Enniscorthy—A large town located in County Wexford and the site of many battles during the 1798 Rebellion.

Wexford—The county town of County Wexford and site of many key events during the 1798 Rebellion.

Barrow—The River Barrow, the longest of the three rivers known as the Three Sisters.

Ross—The Wexford town of New Ross, where the rebels were gravely defeated, halting the spread of the rebellion into County Kilkenny.

Brave Harvey—Beauchamp Bagenal Harvey, commander of the United Irishmen at the Battle of New Ross, later executed by the British.

Slaney—The River Slaney in southeast Ireland.

Mount Leinster—A mountain straddling the border between Counties Carlow and Wexford.

SELECTED RECORDINGS

The Clancy Brothers & Tommy Makem,
Kelly the Boy from Killane (1956)

Don Partridge, *Kelly the Boy from Killane* (1964)

The Dubliners, *Kelly the Boy from Killane* (1967)

Luke Kelly, *Kelly the Boy from Killane* (2004)

The High Kings, *Kelly the Boy from Killane* (2017)

Irish Poet & Songwriter Thomas Moore

The Minstrel Boy

THE STORY: A young man goes off to war, swearing to fight for freedom while singing the praises of Ireland with his harp. When he is mortally wounded in battle, he destroys his harp rather than let it fall into the hands of the enemy.

The minstrel boy to the war is gone;
In the ranks of death you'll find him;
His father's sword he has girded on,
And his wild harp slung behind him;
"Land of Song!" said the warrior bard,
"Though all the world betrays thee,
One sword, at least, thy rights shall guard,
One faithful harp shall praise thee!"

The Minstrel fell! But the foeman's chain
Could not bring that proud soul under;
The harp he loved ne'er spoke again,
For he tore its chords asunder;
And said, "No chains shall sully thee,
Thou soul of love and bravery!
Thy songs were made for the pure and free
They shall never sound in slavery!"

SONG NOTES & HISTORY

The Minstrel Boy was written by Irish poet Thomas Moore and first published in his 1813 collection *Irish Melodies*. Set to the tune of the air *The Moreen*, it was composed to honor Moore's friends and colleagues who fought in the Irish Rebellion of 1798. The song gained widespread popularity during the U.S. Civil War among Irish soldiers and has since become a favorite of Irish-American police officers and firefighters. It has been featured in numerous films and TV shows, including *Star Trek*, *The Young Indiana Jones Chronicles*, *The Man Who Would Be King*, and *Black Hawk Down*. The song is no. 13,867 in the Roud Folk Song Index.

SELECTED RECORDINGS

Paul Robeson, *The Minstrel Boy* (1954)

The Clancy Brothers & Tommy Makem,
The Minstrel Boy (1956)

Bing Crosby, *The Minstrel Boy* (1961)

IRISH SONGS OF WAR & REBELLION

John McDermott, *The Minstrel Boy* (1992)

The Corrs, *The Minstrel Boy* (1995)

Shane MacGowan & The Popes,
The Minstrel Boy (2001)

Joe Strummer & The Mescaleros,
The Minstrel Boy (2002)

Enter the Haggis, *The Minstrel Boy* (2005)

The Irish Tenors, *The Minstrel Boy* (2010)

Rebel Leader Father Peter Clinch Being Shot at
the Battle of Vinegar Hill, Enniscorthy, Wexford, Ireland

The Rising of the Moon

THE STORY: A young shepherd is told that rebels are gathering at sundown to battle the enemy, presumably the English. The rebels gather their pikes and fight, but are sadly defeated, though others promise to continue the struggle for the freedom of Ireland.

"O then, tell me Sean O'Farrell,
tell me why you hurry so?"
"Hush, *a bhuachaill*, hush and listen,"
And his cheeks were all aglow,
"I bear orders from the Capt'n,
Get you ready quick and soon,
For the pikes must be together,
At the rising of the moon."

By the rising of the moon,
By the rising of the moon,
For the pikes must be together
At the rising of the moon!

"O then, tell me Sean O'Farrell,
Where the gath'rin is to be?"

THE WIND THAT SHAKES THE BARLEY

"In the old spot by the river,
Well known to you and me,
One more word for signal token,
Whistle up the marchin' tune,
With your pike upon your shoulder,
By the rising of the moon."

By the rising of the moon,
By the rising of the moon,
With your pike upon your shoulder,
By the rising of the moon!

Out from many a mud wall cabin
Eyes were watching through the night,
Many a manly heart was beating,
For the blessed morning light.
Murmurs ran along the valleys,
To the banshee's lonely croon,
And a thousand pikes were flashing,
At the rising of the moon.

By the rising of the moon,
By the rising of the moon,
And a thousand pikes were flashing,
At the rising of the moon!

There beside the singing river,
That black mass of men was seen,
High above their shining weapons,
flew their own beloved green.
"Death to every foe and traitor!
Forward! Strike the marching tune.
And hurrah, my boy, for freedom,
'Tis the rising of the moon."

    By the rising of the moon,
    By the rising of the moon,
    And hurrah, my boy, for freedom,
    'Tis the rising of the moon!

Well they fought for poor old Ireland,
And full bitter was their fate,
Oh what glorious pride and sorrow,
Fills the name of ninety-eight!
Yet, thank God, e'en still are beating
Hearts in manhood burning noon,
Who would follow in their footsteps,
At the rising of the moon.

    By the rising of the moon,
    By the rising of the moon,

Who would follow in their footsteps,
At the rising of the moon!

SONG NOTES & HISTORY

Sung to the tune of another popular Irish ballad, *The Wearing of the Green*, this rousing call to arms was first published in 1866 in Fenian poet John Keegan Casey's collection *A Wreath of Shamrocks*. It was written to commemorate the Irish Rebellion of 1798, though the battle and the enemy are never actually named. By all historical accounts, the Sean O'Farrell mentioned in the lyric is not a real person. The song is still popular in Ireland today and is often taught in schools and played at sporting events. It is no. 9634 in the Roud Folk Song Index.

WORDS TO KNOW

A bhuachaill—An old Irish term meaning boy or cowherd.

Banshee—A shrieking spirit in Irish mythology.

SELECTED RECORDINGS

The Clancy Brothers & Tommy Makem,
The Rising of the Moon (1956)

Peter, Paul & Mary, *The Rising of the Moon* (1965)

The Dubliners, *The Rising of the Moon* (1967)

Shane MacGowan & The Popes,
The Rising of the Moon (1994)

The High Kings, *The Rising of the Moon* (2010)

15ᵗʰ Century Shilling of Henry VII

The Saxon Shilling

THE STORY: Ireland's youth are warned against joining the British army despite how alluring it may seem, for soldiering makes them murderous tools of the King's quest for gold and glory rather than fighters for the freedom of their homeland.

Hark! a martial sound is heard—
The march of soldiers, fifing, drumming;
Eyes are staring, hearts are stirr'd—
For bold recruits the brave are coming.
Ribands flaunting, feathers gay—
The sounds and sights are surely thrilling,
Dazzl'd village youths to-day
Will crowd to take the Saxon Shilling.

Ye, whose spirits will not bow
In peace to parish tyrants longer—
Ye, who wear the villain brow,
And ye who pine in hopeless hunger—
Fools, without the brave man's faith—
All slaves and starvelings who are willing
To sell yourselves to shame and death—
Take now that blood-stained Saxon Shilling.

THE WIND THAT SHAKES THE BARLEY

Ere you from your mountains go
To feel the scourge of foreign fever,
Swear to serve the faithless foe
That lures you from your land for ever!
Swear henceforth its tools to be—
To slaughter trained by ceaseless drilling—
Honour, home, and liberty,
Abandon'd for a Saxon Shilling.

Go—to find, 'mid crime and toil,
The doom to which such guilt is hurried;
Go—to leave on Indian soil
Your bones to bleach, accurs'd, unburied!
Go—to crush the just and brave,
Whose wrongs with wrath the world are filling;
Go—to slay each brother slave,
Or spurn the blood-stained Saxon Shilling!

Irish hearts! why should you bleed,
To swell the tide of British glory—
Aiding despots in their greed,
Who've changed our green so oft to gory?
None, but those who wish to see
The noblest killed, the meanest killing,
And true hearts severed from the free,
Will take again the Saxon Shilling!

Irish youths! reserve your strength
Until an hour of glorious duty,
When Freedom's smile shall cheer at length
The land of bravery and beauty.
Bribes and threats, oh, heed no more—
Let naught but justice make you willing
To leave your own dear Island shore,
And never again take a Saxon Shilling.

SONG NOTES & HISTORY

This anti-recruiting ballad was written by Kevin T. Buggy and first published in *The Spirit of the Nation* in 1843. The Saxon shilling is a reference to the payment given to recruits as an enticement to join the British army.

WORDS TO KNOW

Ribands—An archaic spelling of ribbons.

Starveling—An undernourished person.

SELECTED RECORDINGS

The Dubliners, *The Saxon Shilling* (1969)

Sean Tyrell, *The Saxon Shilling* (1995)

Frank Harte & Dónal Lunny, *The Saxon Shilling* (1995)

Irish Revolutionary James Napper Tandy

The Wearing of
the Green

THE STORY: Upon hearing that British authorities have outlawed wearing green clothing and patriotic symbols by punishment of death or torture, an Irish rebel mocks the move for its absurdity. He promises he will continue to celebrate his love of country, even if one day he is driven to leave it.

O Paddy dear, and did you hear
the news that's going round?
The shamrock is forbid by law
to grow on Irish ground;
St. Patrick's Day no more we'll keep;
his colors can't be seen:
For there's a bloody law again'
the wearing of the green.

I met with Napper Tandy,
and he took me by the hand,
And he said, "How's poor old Ireland,
and how does she stand?"
She's the most distressful country
that ever yet was seen:

They are hanging men and women
for the wearing of the green.

Oh, if the color we must wear
is England's cruel red,
Sure Ireland's sons will ne'er forget
the blood that they have shed.
You may take the shamrock from your hat
and cast it on the sod,
But 'twill take root and flourish there,
though under foot 'tis trod.
When law can stop the blades of grass
from growing as they grow,
And when the leaves in summer-time
their verdure dare not show,
Then I will change the color
I wear in my caubeen;
But till that day, please God, I'll stick
to wearing of the green.

But if at last our color should
be torn from Ireland's heart,
Her sons with shame and sorrow from
the dear old isle will part:
I've heard a whisper of a country
that lies beyond the sea,

Where rich and poor stand equal in
the light of freedom's day.
O Erin, must we leave you,
driven by a tyrant's hand?
Must we ask a mother's blessing
from a strange and distant land?
Where the cruel cross of England
shall nevermore be seen,
And where, please God, we'll live and die
still wearing of the green.

SONG NOTES & HISTORY

This street ballad bemoans the repression of the Irish by
the British during the Irish Rebellion of 1798, when the
Society of United Irishmen and their supporters adopted green
as their color. While the title *Wearing of the Green* was first
used on a broadside in the same year as the rebellion, with
many variations of the lyric following after, the most famous
version was written by Dion Boucicault in 1864. The melody
is an old Irish air that has been used for numerous songs,
including *The Rising of the Moon*. In chapter five of the book

Gone with the Wind, Gerald O'Hara sings the ballad on his way to the Twelve Oaks plantation. The song is no. 3278 in the Roud Folk Song Index.

WORDS TO KNOW

Napper Tandy—A reference to James Napper Tandy, a member of the United Irishmen who was exiled after the failed rebellion.

Caubeen—An Irish beret worn by peasants and soldiers.

Erin—The Irish word for Ireland.

SELECTED RECORDINGS

John McCormack, *The Wearing of the Green* (1904)

Judy Garland, *The Wearing of the Green* (1940)

Patrick O'Malley, *The Wearing of the Green* (1961)

The Kelly Family, *The Wearing of the Green* (1979)

The Wolfe Tones, *The Wearing of the Green* (1985)

Orthodox Celts, *The Wearing of the Green* (1997)

A British Army Attack on the Wexford Rebels, 1798

The Wind That Shakes the Barley

THE STORY: A young man is torn between staying with his true love or fighting in the rebellion. When his true love is killed by a shot from an English rifle, he buries her and vows vengeance though he knows it will most certainly mean his own untimely end.

I sat within a valley green,
I sat there with my true love,
My sad heart strove the two between,
The old love and the new love,
The old for her, the new that made
Me think of Ireland dearly,
While soft the wind blew down the glade
And shook the golden barley.

Twas hard the woeful words to frame
To break the ties that bound us,
Twas harder still to bear the shame
Of foreign chains around us,
And so I said, "The mountain glen
I'll seek next morning early,

THE WIND THAT SHAKES THE BARLEY

And join the brave United Men!"
While soft winds shook the barley.

While sad I kissed away her tears,
My fond arms 'round her flinging,
The foeman's shot burst on our ears
From out the wildwood ringing,
A bullet pierced my true love's side
In life's young spring so early,
And on my breast in blood she died
While soft winds shook the barley!

I bore her to the wildwood screen,
And many a summer blossom
I placed with branches thick and green
Above her gore-stain'd bosom,
I wept and kissed her pale, pale cheek,
Then rushed o'er vale and far lea,
My vengeance on the foe to wreak
While soft winds shook the barley!

But blood for blood without remorse,
I've ta'en at Oulart Hollow
And placed my true love's clay-cold corpse
Where I full soon will follow,

And round her grave I wander drear,
Noon, night and morning early,
With breaking heart whene'er I hear
The wind that shakes the barley!

SONG NOTES & HISTORY

This ballad, which resembles the traditional song *The Maid That Sold Her Barley* in meter and tune, was written by Limerick-born poet Robert Dwyer Joyce and published in his 1872 collection *Ballads of Irish Chivalry*. The young man in the song is a Wexford rebel debating whether to join the Irish Rebellion of 1798. The mentions of barley refer to the provisions of oats and barley the Irish rebels carried in their pockets while marching. When the rebellion failed, many of the rebels were executed and buried in mass graves, which for years were marked by the barley that would sprout from the dead men's pockets. Set during the Irish War of Independence, Ken Loach's film *The Wind That Shakes the Barley* won the Palme d'Or at the 2006 Cannes Film Festival. The song is no. 2994 in the Roud Folk Song Index.

WORDS TO KNOW

United Men—The Society of United Irishmen, a revolutionary Republican organization that began the Irish Rebellion of 1798.

Oulart Hollow—A site near Oulart Hill, where Irish rebels massacred a detachment of North Cork militia.

SELECTED RECORDINGS

The Clancy Brothers & Tommy Makem,
The Wind That Shakes the Barley (1956)

Martin Carthy,
The Wind That Shakes the Barley (1965)

Sarah Makem,
The Wind That Shakes the Barley (1968)

Dead Can Dance,
The Wind That Shakes the Barley (1993)

Dick Gaughan,
The Wind That Shakes the Barley (2002)

Loreena McKennitt,
The Wind That Shakes the Barley (2010)

THE KANDYAN WARS

1803-1818

The Kandyan Wars, also known as the Kandian Wars, were a series of conflicts between British colonial forces and the Kingdom of Kandy, an independent monarchy of the island of Sri Lanka. Aided by the surrounding mountainous terrain, the Kandyans fiercely resisted colonization, frustrating British forces for more than a decade until the British finally captured the kingdom in 1815, ending its 400-year reign. Though several smaller uprisings occurred in the years that followed, none was any serious threat to the Crown.

Major Davey's Tree in Ceylon,
the Site of a Massacre of British Soldiers

Johnny I Hardly Knew Ye

THE STORY: A woman encounters the delinquent father of her child and learns he left her to be a soldier. She is surprised to see he has lost his legs, arms, and eyes fighting on the island of Ceylon. Fearing he will become a beggar, she welcomes him home then pledges that no more of Ireland's youth will be sent away to war.

While goin' the road to sweet Athy,
　Hurroo, hurroo!
While goin' the road to sweet Athy,
　Hurroo, hurroo!
While goin' the road to sweet Athy,
A stick in me hand and a drop in me eye,
A doleful damsel I heard cry,
Johnny, I hardly knew ye.

　With your guns and drums and drums and guns,
　　Hurroo, hurroo!
　With your guns and drums and drums and guns,
　　Hurroo, hurroo!

With your guns and drums and drums and guns,
The enemy nearly slew ye,
Oh my darling dear, ye look so queer,
Johnny, I hardly knew ye.

Where are your eyes that were so mild,
    Hurroo, hurroo!
Where are your eyes that were so mild,
    Hurroo, hurroo!
Where are your eyes that were so mild,
When my heart you so beguiled?
Why did ye skedaddle from me and the child?
Oh Johnny, I hardly knew ye.

With your guns and drums and drums and guns,
    Hurroo, hurroo!
With your guns and drums and drums and guns,
    Hurroo, hurroo!
With your guns and drums and drums and guns,
The enemy nearly slew ye,
Oh my darling dear, ye look so queer,
Johnny, I hardly knew ye.

Where are your legs that used to run,
    Hurroo, hurroo!

Where are your legs that used to run,
    Hurroo, hurroo!
Where are your legs that used to run,
When you went for to carry a gun,
Indeed your dancing days are done,
Oh Johnny, I hardly knew ye.

    With your guns and drums and drums and guns,
        Hurroo, hurroo!
    With your guns and drums and drums and guns,
        Hurroo, hurroo!
    With your guns and drums and drums and guns,
    The enemy nearly slew ye,
    Oh my darling dear, ye look so queer,
    Johnny, I hardly knew ye.

Ye haven't an arm, ye haven't a leg,
    Hurroo, hurroo!
Ye haven't an arm, ye haven't a leg,
    Hurroo, hurroo!
Ye haven't an arm, ye haven't a leg,
Ye're an armless, boneless, chickenless egg,
Ye'll have to be put with a bowl to beg,
Oh Johnny, I hardly knew ye.

With your guns and drums and drums and guns,
 Hurroo, hurroo!
With your guns and drums and drums and guns,
 Hurroo, hurroo!
With your guns and drums and drums and guns,
The enemy nearly slew ye,
Oh my darling dear, ye look so queer,
Johnny, I hardly knew ye.

I'm happy for to see ye home,
 Hurroo, hurroo!
I'm happy for to see ye home,
 Hurroo, hurroo!
I'm happy for to see ye home,
All from the island of Ceylon,
So low in flesh, so high in bone,
Oh Johnny, I hardly knew ye.

With your guns and drums and drums and guns,
 Hurroo, hurroo!
With your guns and drums and drums and guns,
 Hurroo, hurroo!
With your guns and drums and drums and guns,
The enemy nearly slew ye,
Oh my darling dear, ye look so queer,
Johnny, I hardly knew ye.

They're rolling out the guns again,
    Hurroo, hurroo!
They're rolling out the guns again,
    Hurroo, hurroo!
They're rolling out the guns again,
But they never will take our sons again,
No, they never will take our sons again,
Johnny, I'm swearing to ye.

SONG NOTES & HISTORY

Sung to the same tune as *When Johnny Comes Marching Home*, this song is popular throughout the British Isles and the United States. Though credited to songwriter Joseph B. Geoghehan and first published in 1867, it is suspected to have been written in the late 18th or early 19th century around the time of the Kandyan Wars in Sri Lanka, then known as Ceylon. Once considered a humorous song, it has become an impassioned anti-war song due to its rather bleak content. The song is no. 3137 in the Roud Folk Song Index.

WORDS TO KNOW

Athy—A town in County Kildare at the meeting of the River Barrow and the Grand Canal.

SELECTED RECORDINGS

The Clancy Brothers & Tommy Makem,
Johnny I Hardly Knew Ye (1961)

Joan Baez, *Johnny, I Hardly Knew Yeh* (1993)

The Irish Rovers, *Johnny I Hardly Knew Ye* (2003)

Dropkick Murphys, *Johnny I Hardly Knew Ya* (2007)

Janice Ian, *Johnny I Hardly Knew Ye'* (2007)

Patty Duke, *Johnny I Hardly Knew Ye* (2013)

THE NAPOLEONIC WARS

1804-1815

During the rise and eventual fall of Napoleon Bonaparte in Europe, great numbers of Irishmen fought for the British army and navy. The Duke of Wellington, who led the British in the famous Battle of Waterloo, was himself Irish-born. On the contrary, there were also many Irish Catholics who fought for the French after the exodus from Ireland known as the Flight of the Wild Geese.

A British Recruiting Officer Talking with
a Possible New Recruit

Arthur McBride

THE STORY: On Christmas morning, two Irish cousins out for a seaside stroll are approached by an English recruiting party, who try to woo them into the soldiering life. When the Irishmen refuse, the soldiers become combative, only to find themselves quickly dispatched and humiliated by the proud cousins.

> Out for recreation, being on a tramp,
> We met Sergeant Napper and Corporal Vamp
> And a little drummer intending to camp,
> The day being pleasant and charming.

> "Good morning, good morning," the sergeant did cry.
> "The same to you gentlemen," we did reply,
> Intending no harm but meant to pass by,
> It being on Christmas morning.

> Says he, "My fine fellows, if you will enlist,
> Five guineas in gold I will slip in your fist,
> And a crown in the bargain to kick up a dust
> And to drink to king's health in the morning.

THE WIND THAT SHAKES THE BARLEY

"The soldier he leads a very fine life,
He always is blest with a charming, young wife,
He pays all his debt without sorrow or strife
And always lives pleasant and charming.

"The solder he always is decent and clean
While other poor fellows go dirty and mean,
While other poor fellows go dirty and mean
And sup on burgoo in the morning."

Says Arthur, "You needn't be proud of your clothes;
You have but the lend of them as I suppose,
You dare not change them one night for you know,
If you do, you'll be flogged in the morning.

"Although that we are single and free
We take great delight in our country.
We have no desire strange faces to see,
Although that your offers are charming.

"We have no desire to take your advance,
All hazards and dangers we barter on chance.
You would have no scruples to send us to France
Where we would be shot without warning."

Oh then says the sergeant, "I'll have no such chat,
I neither will take it from spalpeen or brat,
For if you insult me in one other word,
I'll cut off your head in the morning."

Then Arthur and I we soon drew our hods
And scarce gave them time for to draw their own blades
When a trusty shillalah came over their heads
And bade them take that as fair warning.

Their old rusty rapiers that hung by their side
We flung them as far as we could in the tide.
"Oh take them out, devils," cried Arthur McBride,
"And temper their edge in the morning."

Oh the little drummer we flattened his pow,
We made a football of his rowdy dow dow,
Threw it in the tide for to rock or to row
And bade it a tedious returning.

We, having no money, paid them off in cracks
And paid no respect to their two bloody backs,
For we lathered them there like a pair of wet sacks
And left them for dead in the morning.

THE WIND THAT SHAKES THE BARLEY

Oh then to conclude and to finish disputes
We obligingly asked if they wanted recruits,
For we were the lads who would give them hard clout
And bid them look sharp in the morning.

SONG NOTES & HISTORY

First collected around 1840, *Arthur McBride* is found in Ireland, Scotland and England with slight variations. The surname McBride was popular in Donegal, Ireland, where many believe the song originated, though the titular Arthur has never been proven real. Paul Brady, who recorded what is widely considered to be the definitive version, learned it from the book *A Heritage of Songs* by Carrie Grover. The ballad is no. 2355 in the Roud Folk Song Index.

WORDS TO KNOW

Burgoo—A spicy stew.

Spalpeen—A layabout, rascal or ruffian.

Shillalah—A cudgel made of hardwood.

Pow—A slang term for a powdered wig.

Rowdy Dow Dow—An onomatopoeia for drum.

Hods—Another term for shillalah or club.

SELECTED RECORDINGS

Martin Carthy & Dave Swarbrick,
Arthur McBride and the Sergeant (1969)

Planxty, *Arthur McBride* (1973)

Paul Brady & Andy Irvine,
Arthur McBride and the Sergeant (1976)

Bob Dylan, *Arthur McBride* (1992)

Napoléon Bonaparte

Mrs. McGrath

THE STORY: A British recruiting sergeant convinces an Irish woman to send her son off to be a soldier. Upon the son's return from war seven years later, the woman is horrified to learn that he has lost his legs to a cannonball.

"Now, Mrs. McGrath," the sergeant said,
"Would you like to make a soldier out of your son Ted?
With scarlet coat and cockade hat,
Now, Mrs. McGrath, wouldn't you like that?"

Mrs. McGrath stood by the shore,
Waiting for her son for seven years or more,
Till she saw a ship sailing into the bay,
"Here's my son Ted now musha clear the way!"

"Captain dear, where have you been?
Have you been sailing on the Mediterranean?
Have you got news of my son Ted?
Is the poor fellow living or is he dead?"

Then up came Ted without any legs,
Walking on a pair of wooden pegs,

THE WIND THAT SHAKES THE BARLEY

She kissed him a dozen times or two,
"Mother of God, sure it can't be you!"

"Were you drunk or were you blind,
When you left your two fine legs behind?
Or was it walking on the sea,
Took your two fine legs from the knees away?"

"No, I wasn't drunk and I wasn't blind,
When I left my two fine legs behind,
But a cannonball on the fifth of May,
Took my fine legs from the knees away."

"Oh, Teddy McGrath," the widow cried,
"Your fine legs were your mother's pride,
Them stumps of trees won't do at all,
Why didn't you run from the cannonball?"

"All foreign wars I do proclaim,
Between Don John and the King of Spain,
I'd rather have me son as he used to be,
Than the King of France and his whole navy!"

SONG NOTES & HISTORY

Set during the Napoleonic Wars, *Mrs. McGrath* has many names and variations including *Mrs. McGraw, My Son Ted, My Son John,* and *The Sergeant and Mrs. McGrath.* The first written account of the song is from 1876, though there are reports of the song being popular with soldiers during the U.S. Civil War. The battle on the fifth of May is presumed to be the Battle of Fuentes de Oñoro. The song is no. 678 in the Roud Folk Song Index.

WORDS TO KNOW

Musha—An Irish slang word used to express pity.

Don John—Most likely Don John of Austria, Spanish general and bastard son of Philip IV, the King of Spain.

SELECTED RECORDINGS

Burl Ives, *Mrs. McGrath* (1958)

The Belafonte Folk Singers,
The Sergeant and Mrs. McGrath (1958)

Tommy Makem, *Mrs. McGrath* (1961)

THE WIND THAT SHAKES THE BARLEY

The Clancy Brothers, *Mrs. McGrath* (1966)

The Dubliners, *Mrs. McGrath* (1964)

Bruce Springsteen, *Mrs. McGrath* (2006)

John C. Reilly, *My Son John* (2006)

The Imagined Village, *My Son John* (2010)

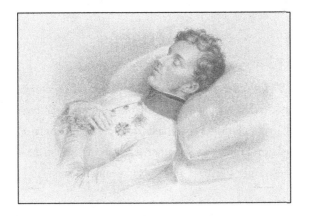

Napoleon II on His Death Bed

The Bonny Bunch
of Roses

THE STORY: Napoleon's son, Napoleon II, promises his mother, the Duchess of Parma, that one day he will continue the fight his father began and take Ireland, England and Scotland for France. His mother warns him against the idea, citing his father's failures in the Napoleonic War.

Near by the swelling ocean,
One morning in the month of June,
While feather'd warbling songsters
Their charming notes did sweetly tune,
I overheard a lady
Lamenting in sad grief and woe,
And talking with young Bonaparte
Concerning the bonny Bunch of Roses, O.

Thus spake the young Napoleon,
And grasp'd his mother by the hand:
"Oh, mother dear have patience,
Till I am able to command;
I'll raise a numerous army,
And through tremendous dangers go,

And in spite of all the universe,
I'll gain the bonny Bunch of Roses, O."

"Oh, son, speak not so venturesome;
For England is the heart of oak;
Of England, Scotland, and Ireland,
The unity can ne'er be broke.
And think you on your father,
In the Island where he now lies low,
He is not yet interred in France;
So beware of the bonny Bunch of Roses, O."

"Your father raised great armies,
And likewise kings did join the throng;
He was so well provided,
Enough to sweep the world along.
But when he went to Moscow,
He was o'erpower'd by drifting snow;
And though Moscow was blazing
He lost the bonny Bunch of Roses, O."

"Oh, mother, adieu for ever,
I am now on my dying bed,
If I had liv'd I'd have been brave
But now I droop my youthful head.
And when our bones do molder,

And weeping-willows o'er us grow,
Its deeds to bold Napoleon
Will stain the bonny Bunch of Roses, O."

SONG NOTES & HISTORY

With its origins in the British Isles, *The Bonny Bunch of Roses* was most likely written by an Irish balladeer, as evidenced by the lyric's sympathetic attitude toward Napoleon's fight against the Crown. The song was first published in William Christie's *Traditional Ballad Airs, Volume II* in 1881 and is no. 664 in the Roud Folk Song Index.

SELECTED RECORDINGS

Paddy Clancy, *Bonny Bunch of Roses-O* (1961)

Fairport Convention, *Bonny Bunch of Roses* (1970)

Shirly & Dolly Collins, *The Bonny Bunch of Roses* (2006)

Norman Blake, Nancy Blake & the Boys of the Lough,
The Bonny Bunch of Roses (2009)

Frank Harte and Dónal Lunny, *Bonny Bunch of Roses* (2009)

Sam Lee & Friends, *Bonny Bunch of Roses* (2015)

THE YOUNG IRELANDER REBELLION

June 29, 1848

Sometimes called the Famine Rebellion, the Battle of Ballingarry or the Rising of 1848, the Young Irelander Rebellion was a failed uprising led by the nationalistic Young Ireland movement. In the village of Ballingarry, South Tipperary, an Irish constabulary unit was chased by a group of Young Irelanders and forced to take refuge in the house of Mrs. Margaret McCormack, whose five children were then taken hostage by the constables. After an hours-long gunfight resulting in the death of two rebels, the Young Irelanders retreated and were later arrested and transported, thereby ending the revolt.

Writer & Young Irelander Thomas Osborne Davis

A Nation Once Again

THE STORY: The narrator proudly proclaims his hope that the people of Ireland will soon rise up, as did so many heroic warriors of old, to free their country from the oppressive rule of the British.

When boyhood's fire was in my blood
I read of ancient freemen,
For Greece and Rome who bravely stood,
Three hundred men and three men;
And then I prayed I yet might see
Our fetters rent in twain,
And Ireland, long a province, be
A Nation once again!

A Nation once again,
A Nation once again,
And Ireland, long a province, be
A Nation once again!

And from that time, through wildest woe,
That hope has shone a far light,

Nor could love's brightest summer glow
Outshine that solemn starlight;
It seemed to watch above my head
In forum, field and fane,
Its angel voice sang round my bed,
A Nation once again!

A Nation once again,
A Nation once again,
And Ireland, long a province, be
A Nation once again!

It whisper'd too, that freedom's ark
And service high and holy,
Would be profaned by feelings dark
And passions vain or lowly;
For, Freedom comes from God's right hand,
And needs a Godly train;
And righteous men must make our land
A Nation once again!

A Nation once again,
A Nation once again,
And Ireland, long a province, be
A Nation once again!

So, as I grew from boy to man,
I bent me to that bidding,
My spirit of each selfish plan
And cruel passion ridding;
For, thus I hoped some day to aid,
Oh, can such hope be vain?
When my dear country shall be made
A Nation once again!

SONG NOTES & HISTORY

First published in 1844, *A Nation Once Again* was written by Thomas Osborne Davis, one of the founders of the Young Ireland nationalist movement. The "three hundred men" mentioned in the first verse are thought to be the Spartans who fought at Thermopylae, while the "three men" are most likely the Roman triplet warriors, the Horatii. During World War II, Winston Churchill famously quoted the song title when unsuccessfully trying to convince Ireland to join forces with Britain. Several years later the song was featured in the Beatles' film *A Hard Day's Night*, as sung by Paul McCartney's grandfather, who declares himself a soldier of the Republic.

SELECTED RECORDINGS

John McCormack, *A Nation Once Again* (1906)

The Clancy Brothers & Tommy Makem,
A Nation Once Again (1961)

The Dubliners, *A Nation Once Again* (1967)

The Wolfe Tones, *A Nation Once Again* (1972)

The Irish Tenors, *A Nation Once Again* (2001)

The Kilkennys, *A Nation Once Again* (2018)

The Famine in Ireland — A Funeral at Skibbereen

Skibbereen

THE STORY: A child asks his father why he left his home in Ireland. His father explains it was the Irish famine and cruelty of the English that caused him to flee—and also led to his wife's untimely demise. To that, the boy swears to return to Ireland someday for revenge.

O Father dear, I often hear you speak of Erin's Isle,
Her lofty scenes, her valleys green, her mountains
    rude and wild,
They say it is a lovely land wherein a prince might dwell,
Oh why did you abandon it? The reason, to me tell.

O son, I loved my native land with energy and pride,
'Til a blight came o'er my crops, my sheep and cattle died,
My rent and taxes were too high, I could not them redeem,
And that's the cruel reason that I left old Skibbereen.

O well do I remember the bleak December day,
The landlord and the sheriff came to drive us all away,
They set my roof on fire with cursed English spleen,
And that's another reason that I left old Skibbereen.

Your mother too, God rest her soul, fell on the snowy ground,
She fainted in her anguish, seeing the desolation round,
She never rose, but passed away from life to mortal dream,
And found a quiet grave, my boy, in dear old Skibbereen.

And you were only two years old and feeble was your frame,
I could not leave you with my friends, you bore your
    father's name,
I wrapped you in my cothamore at the dead of night unseen,
And heaved a sigh and bade good-bye to dear old Skibbereen.

O Father dear, the day may come when in answer to the call,
Each Irishman, with feeling stern, will rally one and all,
I'll be the man to lead the van beneath the flag of green,
When loud and high, we'll raise the cry:
    "Remember Skibbereen!"

SONG NOTES & HISTORY

Known as *Skibbereen, Dear Old Skibbereen, Farewell to Skibbereen* and many other names, this song details the ravages that resulted from the Young Irelander Rebellion of 1848. The song was first published in the 1880 publication *The Irish Singer's Own Book*, in which it was attributed to poet and Skibbereen native Patrick Carpenter. It was first recorded by John Avery Lomax in a collection of field recordings of Irish immigrants in Michigan and later revived by Irish singer Joe Heaney in the 1950s. The song was also featured in the film *Michael Collins*, as sung by Liam Neeson. It is no. 2320 in the Roud Folk Song Index.

WORDS TO KNOW

Erin's Isle—The island of Ireland.

Skibbereen—A town in County Cork hard hit by Ireland's Great Famine.

Cothamore—An overcoat.

SELECTED RECORDINGS

O.J. Abbott, *Skibbereen* (1961)

The Dubliners, *Skibbereen* (1967)

The Wolfe Tones, *Skibbereen* (1973)

THE WIND THAT SHAKES THE BARLEY

Sinead O'Connor with The Chieftains,
Skibbereen (1998)

The Merry Ploughboys, *Old Skibbereen* (1999)

Joe Heaney, *Skibbereen* (2000)

Mary Behna Miller, *Skibbereen* (2005)

Irish Stew of Sindidun, *Skibereen* (2015)

THE CRIMEAN WAR

1853-1856

Fought by an alliance of Britain, France, Turkey and Sardinia against Russia, the Crimean War is considered by some to be the first 'world war'. The cause of the conflict was complex, including clashes over the treatment of Christian minorities in the Ottoman Empire, as well as the reluctance of Britain and France to allow Russia to assert control over the Crimean Peninsula. Battles included the 11-month Siege of Sevastopol, the Battle of Alma, and the infamous Charge of the Light Brigade. The war ended with the Treaty of Paris in 1856, after Russia sued for peace, conceding they had no path to victory.

More than 30,000 Irishmen fought in the British army during the war, making up approximately 35-percent of the Crown's forces. Hence the Irish public had a great interest in the war and its outcome.

Irish Republican Charles Joseph Kickham

Glen of Aherlow

THE STORY: Upon the death of his parents and the loss of his family home, an Irishman joins the English army and is sent away to fight. He is blinded in battle and becomes a beggar upon his discharge from service and the end of his pension. He then warns others to think twice before becoming a soldier for England.

My name is Patrick Sheehan,
and my years are thirty-four,
Tipperary is my native place,
not far from Galtymore,
I came of honest parents,
but now they're lying low,
Though many's the pleasant days we spent
in the Glen of Aherlow.

My father died; I closed his eyes,
outside the cabin door,
For the landlord and the sheriff too,
were there the day before,
And then my lovin' mother,
and my sisters three, also,

THE WIND THAT SHAKES THE BARLEY

Were forced to go with broken hearts,
from the Glen of Aherlow.

For three long months, in search of work,
I wandered far and near,
I then went to the poorhouse
to see my mother dear,
The news I heard near broke my heart,
but still in all my woe,
I blessed the friends who made their graves
in the Glen of Aherlow.

Bereft of home and kith and kin,
with plenty all around,
I starved within my cabin,
and slept upon the ground,
But cruel as my lot was,
I never did hardship know,
Till I joined the English army,
far away from Aherlow.

"Rouse up there," cried the corporal,
"Ya lazy Irish hound!
Why don't you hear the bugle,
its call to arms to sound?"

I found I had been dreaming
of the days long, long ago,
And I woke upon Sevastopol,
and not in Aherlow.

I tried to find my musket,
how dark I thought the night!
O blessed God! It wasn't dark,
it was the broad daylight!
And when I found that I was blind,
my tears began to flow,
And I longed for even a pauper's grave
in the Glen of Aherlow.

A poor neglected mendicant,
I wander Dublin's streets
My nine months' pension being out,
I beg from all I meet,
As I joined my country's tyrants,
my face I can never show,
Amongst my dear old neighbors
in the Glen of Aherlow.

So Irish youths, dear countrymen,
take heed in what I say,

For if you join the English ranks,
you'll surely rue the day,
And whenever you're tempted,
a-soldiering to go.
Remember poor blind Sheehan
from the Glen of Aherlow.

SONG NOTES & HISTORY

The Glen of Aherlow, also known as *Patrick Sheehan*, was written by Irish Republican Charles Joseph Kickham and first printed in *The Kilkenny Journal* in 1857. It is based on the true story of Patrick Sheehan, a former British soldier who lost his sight at the Siege of Sevastopol during the Crimean War, and upon his discharge was jailed as a beggar when his pension ended. Sheehan's plight gained notoriety upon the ballad's publication, forcing the British government to release him and award him a lifetime pension. The ballad is no. 983 in the Roud Folk Song Index.

WORDS TO KNOW

Galtymore—A mountain in County Limerick.

Glen of Aherlow—A valley between Slievenamuck Hill and Galtymore in the western part of County Tipperary in Ireland

Sebastopol—Alternate spelling of Sevastopol, a city in Ukraine.

Mendicant—A beggar.

SELECTED RECORDINGS

Joe Heaney, *The Glen of Aherlow* (1964)

Meaití Jó Shéamuis Ó Fátharta,
Patrick Sheehan (2003)

John Kerr, *Patrick Sheehan* (2013)

THE AMERICAN CIVIL WAR

1861-1865

Thousands of Irish-Americans, many of them immigrants who had fled Ireland's Great Famine, served for both the Union and Confederate armies in the American Civil War. It is estimated that 150,000 fought for the North and 20,000 for the South as soldiers, officers and even generals. Perhaps the most famous among them were the 69th New York Infantry Regiment, also known as the Irish Brigade, and the 1st Battalion Virginia Infantry Regulars, both of which suffered great losses in battle.

General Thomas Francis Meagher,
Commander of the Irish Brigade

Paddy's Lament

THE STORY: A man plagued by poverty in Dublin sells his livestock and farm, bids goodbye to his sweetheart, and leaves for America in search of fortune. However, upon his arrival he is drafted into the U.S. Army during the Civil War and promptly loses his leg in battle, a fate he supposes worse than that he would have suffered back in Ireland.

Well, it's by the hush, me boys,
And sure that's to hold your noise,
And listen to poor Paddy's sad narration,
I was by hunger pressed,
And in poverty distressed,
So I took a thought I'd leave the Irish nation.

Here's to you boys, now take my advice,
To America I'll have ye's not be going,
There is nothing here but war,
Where the murderin' cannons roar,
And I wish I was at home in dear old Dublin.

Well, I sold me horse and plough,
My little pigs and sow,

My little plot of land I soon did part with,
And me sweetheart Bid McGee,
I'm afraid I'll never see,
For I left her there that morning broken-hearted.

Well, meself and a hundred more,
To America sailed o'er,
Our fortunes to be made we were thinkin',
When we got to Yankee land,
They shoved a gun into our hands,
Saying "Paddy, you must go and fight for Lincoln."

General Meagher to us he said,
If you get shot or lose your head,
Every murdered soul of youse will get a pension,
Well, meself I lost me leg,
They gave me a wooden peg,
And by God this is the truth to you I mention.

Well, I think meself in luck,
If I get fed on Indian buck,
And old Ireland is the country I delight in,
With the devil, I do say,
It's curse Americay,
For I think I've had enough of your hard fightin'.

THE WIND THAT SHAKES THE BARLEY

SONG NOTES & HISTORY

Also known as *By the Hush*, *By the Hush Me Boys* and *Paddy's Lamentation*, this song was first published around 1870 as a broadside ballad entitled *Pat in America*. The original composer is unknown. It is popular among the Irish immigrant population in Canada, where it was first recorded in 1957 in a field recording by folklorist Edith Fowke. Several lines of the song can be heard in the Martin Scorsese film "Gangs of New York" as sung by folk singer Linda Thompson.

WORDS TO KNOW

Meagher—General Thomas Francis Meagher, commander of the famous 69th New York Infantry Regiment that fought in Fredericksburg and the battle of Richmond.

SELECTED RECORDINGS

O.J. Abbott, *By the Hush, Me Boys* (1961)

Andy M. Stewart, *By the Hush* (1982)

Frank Harte, *By the Hush Me Boys* (1987)

Ian Giles, *By the Hush*
(Paddy's Lamentation) (1997)

Sinead O'Connor, *Paddy's Lament* (2002)

Gallant Sons of Erin, *Pat in America* (2003)

De Dannan, *Paddy's Lamentation* (2013)

Linda Thompson, *Paddy's Lamentation* (2013)

Irish Stew of Sindidun, *Paddy's Lamentation* (2017)

The Union Army Entering Richmond, Virginia, 1865

We Fight for Uncle Sam

THE STORY: An Irish-American soldier joins the famous
"Fighting 69th" to fight for the Union under General George
McClellan. After relating the gory particulars of a victory
against the Confederates, the soldier laments the removal of
McClellan as commander, pleading with President Lincoln to
return the general to the battlefield to lead them.

Well, I am a modern hero:
me name is Paddy Kearney;
Not long ago, I landed
from the bogs of sweet Killarney;
I used to cry out: SOAP FAT!
because that was my trade, sir,
Till I 'listed for a Soldier-boy
with Corcoran's brigade, sir.

For to fight for Uncle Sam;
He'll lead us on to glory, O!
He'll lead us on to glory, O!
To save the Stripes and Stars.

Ora, once in regimentals,
my mind it did bewilder.

143

THE WIND THAT SHAKES THE BARLEY

I bid good-bye to Biddy dear,
and all the darling childher;
Whoo! says I, the Irish Volunteer,
the divil a one afraid is,
Because we've got the soldier bold,
McClellan, for to lead us.

    For to fight for Uncle Sam;
    He'll lead us on to glory, O!
    He'll lead us on to glory, O!
    To save the Stripes and Stars.

We soon got into battle:
we made a charge of bay'nets:
The Rebel blackguards soon gave way:
they fell as thick as paynuts.
Och hone! the slaughter that we made,
by-god, it was delighting!
For, the Irish lads in action are
the divil's boys for fighting.

    They'll fight for Uncle Sam;
    He'll lead us on to glory, O!
    He'll lead us on to glory, O!
    To save the Stripes and Stars.

Och, sure, we never will give in,
in any sort of manner,
Until the South comes back again,
beneath the Starry-Banner;
And if John Bull should interfere,
he'd suffer for it truly;
For, soon the Irish Volunteers
would give him Ballyhooly.

> Oh! they'll fight for Uncle Sam;
> He'll lead us on to glory, O!
> He'll lead us on to glory, O!
> To save the Stripes and Stars.

And! now, before I end my song,
this free advice I'll tender:
We soon will use the Rebels up
and make them all surrender,
And, once again, the Stars and Stripes
will to the breeze be swellin',
If Uncle Abe will give us back
our darling boy McClellan.

> Oh! we'll follow Little Mac;
> He'll lead us on to glory, O!

He'll lead us on to glory, O!
To save the Stripes and Stars.

SONG NOTES & HISTORY

We'll Fight for Uncle Sam was commonly sung to the tune of *Whiskey in the Jar*, one of the oldest and most popular Irish folk songs. The lyric details the exploits of the Fighting 69th New York Infantry Regiment, which was made up mostly of Irish-Americans and suffered the third most casualties of any brigade in the war.

WORDS TO KNOW

Killarney—A town in Ireland's County Kerry.

Corcoran's Brigade—A reference to Irish-born General Michael Corcoran who led the 69th New York Infantry Regiment, also known as the Irish Brigade, until his death in 1863.

Ora— An exclamation of enthusiasm.

McClellan—General George McClellan, commander of the Army of the Potomac, which included the 69th New York Infantry Regiment.

Och, Hone—An exclamation of lamentation.

Give Him Ballyhooly—Similar to "Give him hell" and possibly a reference to the Ballyhooly Massacre during the Irish Civil War.

Uncle Abe—Abraham Lincoln, sixteenth President of the United States of America.

Little Mac— A popular nickname for General McClellan, who had been removed from command by the President for several less than stellar campaigns.

SELECTED RECORDINGS

Jerry Ernst, *We'll Fight for Uncle Sam* (2002)

David Kincaid, *We'll Fight for Uncle Sam* (2003)

Gallant Sons of Erin, *We'll Fight for Uncle Sam* (2003)

Fulwood Barracks, Preston, Lancashire, England

McCafferty

THE STORY: A man named McCafferty pursues his dream of joining the British army, only to develop an antagonistic relationship with his captain. After being charged with neglecting his duty—his punishment being no pay and a two-week confinement to his barracks—McCafferty decides to murder the captain upon their next meeting. However, when the moment comes, he accidentally shoots and kills another officer as well. When McCafferty is sentenced to hang, he warns others against the dishonesty and authoritarianism of the British army.

> When I was eighteen years of age,
> Into the army I did engage,
> I left my home with a good intent,
> For to join the forty-second regiment.
>
> To Fulwood Barracks I did go,
> To spend some time in that depot,
> But out of trouble I never could be,
> Captain Hansen took a great dislike to me.
>
> While I was posted on guard one day,
> Some soldiers' children came out to play,

THE WIND THAT SHAKES THE BARLEY

From the officers' quarters my captain came,
And he ordered me for to take their names.

I took one name instead of three,
On neglect of duty they then charged me,
I was confined to barracks with loss of pay,
For doing my duty the opposite way.

A loaded rifle I did prepare,
For to shoot my Captain in the barracks square,
It was my Captain I meant to kill,
But I shot my Colonel against my will.

At Liverpool Assizes my trial I stood,
And I held my courage as best I could,
Then the old judge said, "Now, McCafferty,
Go prepare your soul for eternity."

I had no father to take my part,
No loving mother to break her heart,
I had one friend and a girl was she,
Who'd lay down her life for McCafferty.

So, come all you officers take advice from me,
And go treat your men with some decency,

For it's only lies and a tyranny,
That have made a murderer of McCafferty.

SONG NOTES & HISTORY

This street ballad tells the true story of Patrick McCaffery—most often wrongly spelled McCafferty in the ballad—an Irish soldier executed in 1862 for the murder of two British officers at Fulwood Barracks in Preston, Lancashire, England. It is no. 1148 in the Roud Folk Song Index and is presumed to have been written in the late 19th century. For decades, many British soldiers believed it be against regulations to sing the song and similar superstitions related to the ballad have likely led to its modest popularity and meager recording history.

WORDS TO KNOW

Fulwood Barracks—A military installation at Fulwood in Preston, Lancashire, England.

Assizes—Periodic civil and criminal courts once held around England and Wales.

SELECTED RECORDINGS

The Dubliners, *McCafferty* (1967)

Bill Smith, *McCaffery* (1980)

Roy Harris, *McCafferty* (1995)

THE FENIAN UPRISING

1867

The Fenian Uprising was organized, albeit poorly, by the radical nationalist Irish Republican Brotherhood in rebellion against British rule. Due to lack of arms, careless planning, and cooperation by informants with British police, the movement had hardly begun before most of its leaders were arrested and imprisoned. Following the arrests, there were a series of failed attempts to free the Fenian prisoners including a London bombing and an attack on a prison van, the latter of which resulted in the accidental murder of a policeman and subsequent execution of three Fenians for the crime.

Fenian Attack on a Police Van in Manchester

God Save Ireland

THE STORY: Three Irishmen are hanged for crimes associated with the fight for Ireland's freedom. Their last words before they are hanged are "God Save Ireland," a mantra that inspires generations of Irish nationalists to follow.

High upon the gallows tree
Swung the noble-hearted three.
By the vengeful tyrant stricken in their bloom;
But they met him face to face,
With the courage of their race,
And they went with souls undaunted to their doom.

"God save Ireland!" said the heroes;
"God save Ireland!" said they all.
Whether on the scaffold high,
Or the battlefield we die,
Oh, what matter when for Erin dear we fall!

Girt around with cruel foes,
Still their courage proudly rose,
For they thought of hearts that loved them far and near;
Of the millions true and brave

THE WIND THAT SHAKES THE BARLEY

O'er the ocean's swelling wave,
And the friends in holy Ireland ever dear.

    "God save Ireland!" said the heroes;
    "God save Ireland!" said they all.
    Whether on the scaffold high,
    Or the battlefield we die,
    Oh, what matter when for Erin dear we fall!

Climbed they up the rugged stair,
Rang their voices out in prayer,
Then with England's fatal cord around them cast,
Close beside the gallows tree,
Kissed like brothers lovingly,
True to home and faith and freedom to the last.

    "God save Ireland!" said the heroes;
    "God save Ireland!" said they all.
    Whether on the scaffold high,
    Or the battlefield we die,
    Oh, what matter when for Erin dear we fall!

Never till the latest day,
Shall the memory pass away,
Of the gallant lives thus given for our land;
But on the cause must go,

Amidst joy and weal and woe,

Till we make our Isle a nation free and grand.

"God save Ireland!" said the heroes;

"God save Ireland!" said they all.

Whether on the scaffold high,

Or the battlefield we die,

Oh, what matter when for Erin dear we fall!

SONG NOTES & HISTORY

This rebel song celebrates the Manchester Martyrs, three members of the Irish Republican Brotherhood who were executed in 1867 for the murder of a police officer in Manchester, England. Their last words were indeed "God Save Ireland." The song was considered the unofficial Irish national anthem by Irish nationalists until early in the 1900s. It was written by Timothy Daniel Sullivan and first published in 1867, the day before the Manchester Martyrs' funeral. To help encourage the song's popularity, it was set to the tune of *Tramp! Tramp! Tramp!*, a well-known Union anthem from the U.S. Civil War.

WORDS TO KNOW

Erin—The Irish word for Ireland.

SELECTED RECORDINGS

The Dubliners, *God Save Ireland* (1969)

The Wolfe Tones, *God Save Ireland* (1969)

Dermot O'Brien, *God Save Ireland* (2008)

ABOUT THE AUTHOR

JOSHUA HAMPTON is a writer who finds his muse in everything from Anglo-Saxon epic poetry to French New Wave cinema. His work has been featured in *Heroic Fantasy Quarterly*, *Aphelion* and *Mirror Dance*, among others. He is also a past editor of the English football club Chelsea's stateside newsletter. Joshua lives with his wife, children, two dogs, and the occasional fish near Louisville, Kentucky. His books are available on Amazon.com and by special order at most bookstores.

To learn more, visit **www.JoshuaHampton.com**

THANK YOU FOR
BUYING THIS BOOK!

I hope you enjoyed *The Wind That Shakes the Barley*. If you did, I would kindly ask you to consider leaving a positive review online. Customer reviews (especially those with five stars!) help with sales, and as an independent author every little bit counts. Just a few words is enough. Even if you didn't buy the book online, you can still post your opinion at most retailers if you have an account.

I really appreciate your support and I look forward to reading your feedback!

Made in the USA
Las Vegas, NV
08 August 2024

93501835R00098